Substance Abuse Symptoms and Highly Successful Proven Alleviation Strategies

Robert E. Bunyard, MS

Copyright © 2023 by Robert E. Bunyard, MS

ISBN:978-1-960224-72-9

All rights reserved. No part of this book may be reproduced or transmitted in any form or by any means, electronic or mechanical, including photocopying, recording, or by any information storage and retrieval system, without permission in writing from the copyright owner.

The views expressed in this work are solely those of the author and do not necessarily reflect the views of the publisher, and the publisher disclaims any responsibility for them.

To order additional copies of this book, contact:
Proisle Publishing Services LLC
39-67 58th 1st Floor Woodside
New York, NY 11377, USA
Phone: (+1 347-922-3779)
info@proislepublishing.com

Contents

I. Seven (7) Sequential Steps to Substance Abuse Alleviation 1

II. Fifteen (15) Warning Signs of Teenage Drug Abuse 12

III. Seven (7) Warning Signs of an Addictive Personality 14

IV. Secrets the American Medical Association (AMA), American Psychological Association (APA), and Federal Drug Administration (FDA) Hope the Consumer (You and I) Never Find Out 17

These seven practical steps to substance abuse alleviation are quite helpful all and/or in part for the arrestment of other addictions, including sexual dysfunction, obesity, gambling, smoking, etc.

I

SEVEN (7) SEQUENTIAL STEPS TO SUBSTANCE ABUSE ALLEVIATION

1. The first and necessarily foremost *solution* is to finally realize and personally accept ownership of the disease concept—"I am a drug and/or alcohol abuser." To continuously deny that alcohol and/or other drugs (legal and illegal) have become a number one priority in one's life will only result in his/her continuance to proceed toward a sad destruction, a true living hell!
2. A second solution overlaps the first in, let us say, a continuous and vigorous ongoing *education* with the distinct mission of combating our disease now that we have finally surrendered our total self to being a member of the *hooked* group. We must realize and accept the fact that there is *no known cure* for our condition, medical wise or otherwise. Now, assuming you do really believe and accept the aforementioned data referred to at the beginning of this paragraph, the next logical sequential step (or solution 3) involves an ongoing healthy and active loving support group or groups.
3. In other words, the third solution necessitates forced positive changes in crucial areas of one's life. Why? Later stages of the progressive disease (alcoholism and/or drug addiction) lead one into a life of uncontrollable unmanageability. Therefore a new perspective concerning new friends and also a new attitude and perspective toward our old significant others is a must! As we start fighting the disease with the ultimate goal of becoming totally abstinent

from our drug usage, we see the solution must demand activation from within. Divine intervention, a higher power, a spiritual awakening as Alcoholics Anonymous I Narcotics Anonymous (AA/NA) refers to in their step-by-step guidance procedures; loved ones' tender loving care and ongoing education on the disease itself; plus a medical realization that since we have been using — then abusing — said drugs for so long, it will take quite a while for the mind and body to be cleansed of these built-up toxins, especially damage to the nervous system. Did you know that the psychological professionals who specialize in drug therapy say that for every year of continuous use of a particular drug choice beginning at onset, it will Take about a month to heal the mind/body? For example, let's say John Doe admits to beginning his alcohol drinking behaviors at the age of fourteen. Now he is twenty-five years of age; 25 - 14 = 11. Therefore, approximately eleven months of continuous abstinence dictates an enriching healthier state of 'mental/emotional stability; including a more genuine positive outlook on all of life's experiences. I am not saying improvement will not begin to be noticeable shortly after making a sincere commitment toward abstinence; it takes a while for the neurons in the nervous system to rid themselves of the addicted drug's residue.

4. Before putting any chemicals (pills, food, beverages, anything) into our system, we should always check the label for actual contents; seek professional advice from our trusted medical doctor, registered nurse, or mental health specialist; and not forget our nearest health food center/market! Garbage in = garbage out, healthy input = healthy output. Plain and simple common sense should never be overlooked!

5. This week, next week, and every week to come, take at least three one-ounce shots of wheatgrass (found at a progressive health food store) instead of three shots of tequila/whiskey. Take at least a daily multivitamin and mineral supplement,

and also walk and/or jog at least three miles per week (each week now) instead of just saying I will or, even worse, feeling low and beginning the (bought process of poor *pitiful* me to the following-up with a mood-altering chemical of some sort to instigate that vicious drug/alcohol abuse cycle all over again today.

6. The third solution touches on the spiritual dimension — divine intervention/a spiritual awakening — to arrest the growth of the drug/alcohol disease progression. A spiritual awakening — that part of each and every one of us on this planet that cannot be found on an x-ray, MRI, EKG, EEG, or any other medical machine — is an absolute must to arrest and stop further natural progression of the disease itself! Again, drug/alcohol abuse is incurable; therefore, a strong inner self commitment to fight this *enemy* and win is a mandatory lifesaving answer and/or remedy.

7. The heart and soul of any society, as far as survival is concerned, starts and ends with the strength of each individual family's structure and/or bond. Let ours be strong with the goal of being stronger. In other words, we should have no less than three family meetings at or near a regular designated time each and every week in the home environment, so each and every member of said household can and will be heard, understood, appreciated, and assisted with any and all of his/her unresolved everyday life dilemmas. Actions do speak louder than words, and/or nonverbal communication is stronger than verbal communication, so do use both!

First Solution

Question 1: What do you mean by the *disease concept* concerning drug/alcohol abuse?

Answer: According to the American Medical Association and most other professional affiliations who are given the authority to diagnose and categorize specific sicknesses; a disease is a permanent condition that is progressive in nature. Therefore it is mandatory that one who is abusing drugs/alcohol realize the problem is defined as a disease, and must be treated as such. To get a client/user to totally accept and believe this concept is the first step in a drug therapy clinic, both in and outpatient. Ironically it is the most difficult concept for the abuser to finally realize!

Question 2: Why is the disease concept nearly impossible to grasp?

Answer: The answer is truly amazing and probably the number one reason drug/alcohol abuse is such a great problem in our society today — the *denial* psychological factor/characteristics of the disease that continuously tells the abuser that they really do not have the problem! Someone/Anyone who has progressively increased usage of said drug/alcohol over a period of time will nearly always attribute the usage to an escape and/or remedy for other situations involving life's conflicts. For example: (Q) Why do you drink alcohol so much Johnny? (A) Well, it helps me to relax my mind from the problems I'm facing at school, with my parents, and a few other situations that have occurred lately. This again is a characteristic of the *denial* factor.

SECOND SOLUTION

Question 1: Let's say we finally *see* the *light,* so to speak, and break denial of the disease. Are we cured of alcoholism/drug addiction?

Answer: *No!* You see there is no cure for this disease. Therefore a challenging goal moving in the direction of total abstinence is the ultimate arrestment prescription. Sound easy? Far, far from it! Our society alone reinforces susceptibility to drug dependencies in so many different ways, including over the-counter drugs, MD prescriptions, liquor stores, etc. I am not insinuating this aforementioned list is altogether wrong and/or at fault, but one who has the disease must be extra careful as to his/her selection of usage

Question 2: How do we stop this drug abuse cycle then?

Answer: A vigorous and continuous lifelong education on our disease plus a positive and healthy support group will go a long way toward arrestment, even a *kind of cure,* as long as we do not go back to using, as stresses mount in everyday life situations.

    A total commitment to one's own therapy strategy to avoid mood-altering chemicals dictates a constant awareness of one's situation, by staying abreast of any/ all educational materials related to drug/alcohol use and abuse. The more we know, the better we can combat the urge.

THIRD SOLUTION

Question 1: What is meant by one's own therapy strategy in avoiding further drug/alcohol abuse?

Answer: Now that one admitted to being a member of the *hooked* group, he/she needs to rethink and re-act daily routines in avoidance of the previous lifestyle centered around drug/ alcohol intake. Two comforting, understanding, emphatic, and combatants of the disease are Alcoholics Anonymous and Narcotics Anonymous groups. These are self-supporting with a "one day (twenty-four hours) at a time" strategy leading to long-term sobriety. One must always be aware that for every month/year since first intake of specific abused chemical, it may very well take quite a while for the body and mind to rid itself of the poison toxins and their buildup in our system; especially t lie neurotoxins in and out nervous system!

Question 2: If we are successfully addressing our drug/alcohol problem and are sold on the goal of total abstinence, what are realistic expectations and results of our efforts?

Answer: As I mentioned in the third solution section, for every year that one has used said drugs of choice, starting with the very first experience, subtract that year from present date (Today). This is a good general rule of thumb for the body to clear of practically all the toxins. Also along the way, day by day, one will (slowly at first thought) begin to notice that he/she is feeling better, healthier, happier and more at ease within himself/herself with their external surrounding—a new beginning so to speak.

FOURTH SOLUTION

Question 1: What is so profound about solution #4

Answer: Sometimes we are all guilty of overlooking simple common sense factors as to consumption into our precious bodies, especially today in this rush, rush fast food society. To not be more cautious about any and all substances (food, pills, beverage, other solutions, etc.) we put into our system, can mean severe consequences sooner or later; especially for those who are true drug/alcohol abusers wanting seriously to recover.

Question 2: What do you mean by saying the health food store professional can inadvertently aid in combating alcohol/drug abuse?

Answer: An MD is, for all practical purposes, a human chemist. The doctor treats our illness symptoms by medication and/or extraction. I myself have had a long-term depression problem that finally was solved by finding out at a health food store that I was not ingesting enough folic acid, and guess what, my depression disappeared! You can find even better and much less expensive alternatives to mind/body dysfunctions, on many occasions, at the health food stores instead of via pharmaceuticals.

FIFTH SOLUTION

Question 1: Why is wheatgrass considered a remedy?

Answer: A drug/alcohol abuser, in recovery mode especially, needs to drastically switch unhealthy drug/alcohol chemistry intake for a healthier drug intake. Wheatgrass is an excellent start as a cleanser and natural disposer of unclean toxins in our body. Just go to the health food store and check it out. Later, we will go into it more specifically if you wish. Bottom line is, it works for everyone and not just abusers, per se; along the same principle, we regularly service our own private vehicle in the way of oil changes, transmission oil changes, and coolant system changes.

Question 2: Are you saying to jog/walk three miles a week, every week, will arrest alcohol/drug abuse?

Answer: To arrest this deadly disease mandates a complete lifestyle and priorities adjustment! It is so ironic that these readjustments will also greatly improve every living souls overall mental and physical health!

SIXTH SOLUTION

Question 1: What do you mean by a *spiritual awakening*?

Answer: Let us say that one has already broken the denial, psychological symptom of drug/alcohol abuse (*and most don't*); then at this point, he/she realizes that since mankind has no known cure for said disease, an arrestment procedure leading toward abstinence must come from supernatural force/s. This realm of spirituality (or religiosity to many) is necessary to cope with the ongoing disease progression. One's inner spiritual strength shall and will overcome the need for the chemical abuser's intake and ultimate inappropriate behaviors that were once the accepted practice.

In other words, to admit total defeat by the disease in the way of acceptance of its permanent presence; one is activating an inner strength found on no medical machine that can and will lead to a more productive, healthy, and wonderful life; if and when accepted and practiced twenty-four hours each and every day. This is a building process, needless to say!

Question 2: Define/explain spiritual dimension/divine intervention.

Answer: Years ago, I had a football coach in high school who told us (the team) that success/ winning was 99 percent perspiration and 1 percent inspiration/ Dueling with one of, of not the most devastating problems in our society (drug/alcohol abuse) necessitates knowing and preparing every known angle to prevent its spread and/or reoccurrence. Therefore, the world in and outside of the physical dimension — the spiritual dimension — must be relied upon to continue our existence. Remember, there is no medical/physical world cure.

Regardless of one's religious faith and convictions, the power within or shining light to our soul must be ignited. Whether one is or is not drug dependent, each of us should at least attend an AA or NA meeting, a codependency meeting on substance abuse, and/or a formal drug prevention FED/STATE/SCHOOL oriented program (at least once or twice)!

SEVENTH SOLUTION

Question 1: Since I have the disease, does it affect in my family and elsewhere?

Answer: Drug/Alcohol abuse is referred to in, inpatiend drug rehabilitation hospitals, is categorized under the topic of chemical dependency. A vital and major part of the treatment plan and procedure involves at least one, sometimes two family meetings each week to educate the significant others on the dependency issues. Why? It is considered a family problem, not just a member's problem. The team concept is a must! The stronger and closer the family bond, the better the chances of full recovery!

Question 2: Is there a light at the end of the tunnel on this topic of chemical dependency?

Answer: *Yes,* but not until we, as a society, finally get out of denial and quit trying to hide the problem in the closet or under the rug. To change the overall attitude involving strategies (including the fact that it is a disease, not a moral issue, per se) will make us all stronger first as a family and then moreover as a nation overall.

Research tells us that one-tenth or one out of every ten of us who use mood-altering chemicals do not process the chemicals normally within the body. If we take this statistic as valid and reliable, plus realize that an average family size in the USA is, say, five members; we have nearly every other household on the block needing to actively deal with this astounding dilemma. Who of us cannot afford to get involved?

II

Fifteen (15) Warning Signs of Teenage Drug Abuse

1. High school course material dropping two (2) letter grades
2. Unexplained missing doses from the medicine cabinet relating to prescription and/or OTC drugs in the home environment, usually located in the bathroom.
3. Developing pattern of being home late from social gatherings involving peers.
4. A noticeable lack of interest and enthusiasm in areas he/she once adored.
5. Not enough quality TLC with parents one-to-one, plus family meetings beyond the dinner table.
6. Noticeable and moreover unnoticeable decline in healthy goal oriented leisure time.
7. Increasing tardiness and decreasing school class attendance
8. Parent(s) denial that their son/daughter may be using drugs
9. Teenager's denial as well
10. Lack of at least an incomplete ongoing drug/alcohol related educational program in the home first of all, then also at school, and even in the religious setting.
11. Drug oriented role models, or implications thereof
12. Lack of honest and sincere informative and persistent sex education program in the home and school settings.

13. Not enough planned outings mandatory for all family members to attend.
14. Weak religious convictions
15. Poor overall family team concept

III

SEVEN (7) WARNING SIGNS OF AN ADDICTIVE PERSONALITY

An intense competitive nature to win (regardless of the obstacles, the price, the pain and suffering) is considered one of if not the most admirable traits for one to possess in our modern society and has been for many decades, but in an increasing fashion. As this *super* goal-oriented focus develops and again intensifies from childhood through adulthood, the will to win regarding work-related activities, sibling rivalry, sports, other family relations, etc. can also be counter-productive for many. Being extremely competitive in all aspects of life may very well lend itself to abnormal drug/alcohol use, as in being the life of the party at social gatherings by out-doing others in the beverage consumption department. This behavior whether conscious or unconscious, may lead to a darker side of the aforementioned trait of ultimate sacrifice at whatever the cost!

An individual's highly programmed attitude/mindset that suggests: *Good is not enough.* Extra effort always brings added reward/satisfaction and other inner motivators to deal with all areas of life's tasks may consequently be setting oneself up for devastation when failure/s occur along the way.

Daily life dictates numerous struggles, pressures, strains, and other excessive physical and mental breakdowns just to exist. Do we take enough time each day also to relax, recuperate, and reenergize? Herein lies our answer to healthy balance or unhealthy addictive tendencies. What are yours?

Subtle, then more abrupt, changes in one's priorities as a result of seeking *rushes*, thrills, added relaxation, plus overall immediate gratification may be triggering more in-depth uncontrollable urges leading to addictive behavior.

One's own innermost definition of the term *moderation* as compared to the AMA and APA definitions gives a pretty accurate barometer concerning his/her susceptibility to addictive behavior. Think about it!

Our physical bodies have certain specific needs to function: food, water, vitamins, minerals, etc. Our mental and spiritual well-being includes a certain degree of positive interactions with significant- others, a healthy self-image, high self-esteem, and self-confidence to include supernatural forces of a sort. These needs, at the very least, aid in our making decisions (both voluntarily and involuntarily) that determine our stability in everyday life situations.

Our wants many times are even greater to activate purpose and long-range goal strategies for accomplishments and/or personal achievement. If and when our wants/desires become too deviated beyond our basic needs; herein lies roots for unhealthy levels of frustration, disappointment, depression, excess anxiety, that leads to addictive usage of mood-altering chemicals to deal with said needs vs want imbalances.

Research has shown that genetic tendencies are a factor to consider in assessing one's *addictive* potential. Do medical histories of parents and other family members of past generations disclose addictions?

The other major factor in considering one's tendency toward addictive behavior relates to his/her own living environment. A potentially addictive personality would tend to live in closer proximity to wanted *escapes* (i.e., gaming locales, known accesses to drug activity, excessive party environments) to feel comforting security when hard times become a reality.

IV

Secrets the American Medical Association (AMA), American Psychological Association (APA), and Federal Drug Administration (FDA) Hope the Consumer (You and I) Never Find Out

Did you know that a physician is really just an expert professional limn.in chemist? We get sick, go to the doctor, get a pill, liquid solution, shot, and/or surgery to remove a part of our anatomy. Now, other than the surgery, our medical profession and especially the pharmaceutical companies would go out of business! So we treat the symptoms instead of the cause. The symptoms disappear for a period of time and then reappear at a later date.

If we, the consumer, were programmed (educate fully and properly) for our total best interest, we would not need to see a MD nearly as much, and probably not need such high medical premiums to live a more completely happy and healthy life.

Since our body is a chemical organism; by applying the correct chemical intake, we should obviously cut down on unneeded materials that poison our system(s). I'm sure you have heard over and over again that diet and exercise will alleviate many internal breakdowns. This is very true! However, the media, (especially pharmaceutical commercials) AMA, APA, FDA, and our modern American culture that pressed all of us to have what we want *now*.

This fast-food, fast-buck philosophy keeps us stressed out to the extent that we do not take the much needed time each day to recuperate. The big business capitalistic corporations, including the *feds*, of course would be in more ruin, if we all decided to listen to the health food professional at the local health food store instead of the multibillion-dollar pill-pushing industry!

www.ingramcontent.com/pod-product-compliance
Lightning Source LLC
LaVergne TN
LVHW050027080526
838202LV00069B/6956